# Joan Didion

Navigating Truth, Memory, and Myth

**Henry Will Clarke**

JOAN DIDION

NAVIGATING TRUTH, MEMORY,
AND MYTH

HENRY WILL CLARKE

# Table of Contents

# Preface

This book is a journey into the life and work of Joan Didion—a writer whose incisive observations, masterful prose, and fearless exploration of the human condition have left an indelible mark on American literature. Didion's writing transcends simple storytelling; it is a relentless quest for truth, a dissection of the myths that shape our society, and a meditation on the very act of living. In her own words,

> *"I write entirely to find out what I'm thinking, what I'm looking at, what I see and what it means."*

These words encapsulate the spirit of her creative process—a process that was as much about self-discovery as it was about chronicling the external world.

In these pages, you will find a comprehensive exploration of Didion's multifaceted career. We begin with her deep roots in Sacramento and the formative influence of California—a landscape that not only nurtured her early dreams but also provided the mythic backdrop for her later work. Her education at Berkeley and the transformative experience at *Vogue* set her on a path toward a writing style that is both elegant and uncompromisingly honest. Through her early essays, novels, and screenplays, Didion redefined journalism and fiction, blending personal narrative with cultural critique in a manner that was as innovative as it was influential.

Her landmark collection, *Slouching Towards Bethlehem*, stands as a testament to her role as a pioneering force in New Journalism, where she captured the disjointed pulse of the 1960s with both clinical detachment and raw emotion. As she famously observed,

*"We tell ourselves stories in order to live."*

This profound insight not only guided her writing but also continues to resonate with readers, inviting us to question the narratives that shape our own lives.

The book also delves into the personal dimensions of Didion's life—her intimate diary entries, post-therapy notes, and reflections on family ties—which reveal a writer unafraid to expose her vulnerabilities. Her memoirs, such as *The Year of Magical Thinking* and *Blue Nights*, confront grief head-on, transforming personal loss into a universal exploration of memory and mortality.

Moreover, the collaborative legacy she forged with her husband, John Gregory Dunne, is celebrated as a vital component of her creative output. Their partnership in film and literature exemplifies how the interplay of personal and professional can yield works that challenge and redefine cultural boundaries.

Finally, this volume examines the enduring impact of Didion's work on American letters. Her precise, often poetic command of language, and her unyielding commitment to capturing the elusive truths of life, have inspired countless writers and thinkers. Her legacy is not static but an ongoing conversation—a dialogue between the past and the present, between memory and myth.

As you read this book, we invite you to explore the vast tapestry of Joan Didion's world—a world where every sentence is crafted with deliberate care, where the personal becomes a lens for understanding society, and where storytelling remains an act of both survival and defiance.

# Chapter 1: Beginnings and Formative Years

## Sacramento Roots and Family Heritage

Joan Didion was a fifth-generation Californian, and her deep connection to the Golden State was more than just geographical—it was woven into her identity, her writing, and her worldview. Born on December 5, 1934, in Sacramento, California, Didion was raised in a family with deep historical roots in the state. Her ancestors had crossed the country in a wagon train during the westward expansion, a legacy of resilience and ambition that would later influence her literary sensibilities.

Didion often reflected on this heritage, recognizing how it shaped her perspective on California, America, and history itself. In her memoir *Where I Was From*, she examined the myths and realities of her home state, deconstructing the romanticized notions of pioneering and self-reliance. "The entire world was framed for me in the context of

California," she wrote, "and specifically in the context of my family's passage to it."

Sacramento in the 1930s and 1940s was a place of tradition and conservatism, where agriculture and state politics shaped daily life. Didion's father, Frank Reese Didion, was involved in finance, while her mother, Eduene Didion, upheld the family's historical legacy. As a child, Joan spent hours in the Sacramento Public Library, devouring books that would later influence her own sharp, unflinching prose.

Despite the idyllic setting, Didion was aware of the illusions that California—and by extension, America—created for itself. "We tell ourselves stories in order to live," she famously wrote in *The White Album*, a line that captured her lifelong examination of narratives, both personal and collective.

Her Sacramento upbringing gave her a front-row seat to the contradictions of the American Dream. She grew up among people who believed in hard work, self-sufficiency, and the promise of the West, yet she would go on to critique those very ideals in her essays and novels. As she put it, "To shift the structure of a family is to shift the structure of a world."

Didion's heritage wasn't just a backdrop—it was an essential force that shaped her literary voice. From her early years in Sacramento to her later dissections of California's culture and politics, her writing always carried the weight of history. Her family's journey westward, their dreams and their disillusionments, became the foundation for one of America's greatest literary chroniclers.

## Education at Berkeley and the Vogue Breakthrough

Joan Didion's journey as a writer truly began at the University of California, Berkeley, where she studied English literature. Though she had always been an avid reader—spending much of her childhood in the Sacramento Public Library—Berkeley exposed her to new literary perspectives, sharpening the precision that would define her writing.

She was an outsider in many ways, something she acknowledged in her characteristic, self-aware tone. "I was one of those children," she later wrote, "who liked to make up stories, who lived in the world of the imagination." But while she was drawn to fiction, it was the discipline of structured prose—essays, criticism, journalism—that would become her defining craft.

At Berkeley, Didion was particularly influenced by the Modernist writers she studied, absorbing the clarity and economy of Hemingway, the skepticism of Eliot, and the cool detachment of Fitzgerald. "Grammar is a piano I play by ear," she once wrote, describing her instinctual grasp of language.

## *Vogue*: The Breakthrough

Didion's path from academia to professional writing took an unexpected turn when, in her senior year, she won an essay contest sponsored by *Vogue* magazine. The prize? A coveted job in New York City as a research assistant. This marked the beginning of her immersion into the world of fashion, culture, and high society journalism.

At *Vogue*, Didion learned the art of concise, stylish writing. "You have to keep the reader moving," she once said about her time there. The magazine's meticulous approach to language, where every word had to earn its place, trained her to wield prose like a scalpel.

She quickly rose through the ranks, becoming an associate features editor and publishing articles that blended cultural observation with literary elegance. But *Vogue* also exposed her to the performative nature of glamour and success. "Style is character," she noted, a phrase that captured both her personal philosophy and the ethos of the publication.

Though her years at *Vogue* immersed her in the polished, sophisticated world of New York media, she remained skeptical of artifice. The detachment and precision she developed during this time would later define her groundbreaking essays and novels. "Writers are always selling somebody out," she famously wrote, a reflection of her ability to look beyond surface appearances and tell the deeper truth beneath them.

Didion's time at Berkeley and *Vogue* set the stage for her evolution as a writer. She had honed her voice, learned the discipline of editing, and developed the sharp observational skills that would make her one of America's most celebrated essayists. New York had refined her, but California was still in her bones—and soon, she would return to dissect it with the clarity and unflinching honesty that would become her trademark.

## Early Influences and the Birth of Her Literary Identity

Joan Didion's literary identity was shaped long before she became one of the most distinctive voices in American letters. Her early influences—both literary and personal—set the foundation for the cool, unsentimental prose and razor-sharp observations that would define her career.

### The Power of Storytelling in Childhood

Born in 1934 in Sacramento, Didion grew up in a household where storytelling was second nature. Her family's deep California roots stretched back to the pioneer days, and she was raised on tales of resilience and survival. This legacy of independence and self-reliance infused her worldview, particularly in how she understood the West's mythology.

As a child, she was an obsessive reader, consuming whatever books were available. "I wrote stories from the time I was five," she later recalled. "I don't know what I assumed would happen to them." She devoured the works of Ernest Hemingway, Henry James, and Joseph Conrad, writers whose precision and restraint would leave a lasting imprint on her own style.

One book, in particular, had a profound impact on her: Hemingway's *A Farewell to Arms*. "When I first read it at 12, I was knocked out by the sentences," she said. "I wanted to figure out how they worked." Hemingway's spare, declarative style and his ability to create mood through understatement became hallmarks of her own prose.

**The Influence of California's Landscape**

Didion's early years in Sacramento also played a crucial role in shaping her literary sensibilities. The vast, open landscapes of California—its arid heat, its gold-hued light, and its ever-present sense of impermanence—became recurring themes in her work. She often wrote about the way geography influences psychology, once noting, "A place belongs forever to whoever claims it hardest, remembers it most obsessively."

This attachment to California was not just sentimental; it was analytical. She was fascinated by how the state's history and mythology shaped its identity, an obsession that would later fuel her works like *Slouching Towards Bethlehem* and *Where I Was From*.

**Developing Her Voice: The Transition from Dreamer to Observer**

While her early love of storytelling was instinctive, it wasn't until her time at the University of California, Berkeley, that she began refining her craft with discipline. "Grammar is a piano I play by ear," she once wrote, highlighting her intuitive yet precise approach to language.

At *Vogue*, where she started her career, Didion learned the importance of brevity and clarity. Writing fashion copy and cultural essays taught her how to be meticulous with words, a skill that would serve her well as she transitioned into more serious journalism and fiction.

But even as she wrote about fashion and celebrity culture, Didion never lost her outsider's gaze. She was always observing, always questioning. "Writers are always selling somebody out," she famously remarked—a recognition of the tension between storytelling and truth.

Her early influences—her family's storytelling, Hemingway's economy of language, California's stark beauty, and the discipline of editorial writing—all converged to shape the voice that would make Joan Didion one of the most revered writers of her time. She had found her literary identity: unsentimental yet deeply evocative, detached yet profoundly personal. And from this foundation, she would go on to redefine American nonfiction.

# Chapter 2: The Emergence of a Distinctive Voice

## Pioneering New Journalism: "Slouching Towards Bethlehem"

By the time *Slouching Towards Bethlehem* was published in 1968, Joan Didion had already distinguished herself as one of the sharpest observers of American culture. But this collection of essays, particularly its title piece, cemented her status as a defining voice of the New Journalism movement—a style that blurred the lines between traditional reporting and literary storytelling.

### The New Journalism Approach

Didion's writing in *Slouching Towards Bethlehem* was unlike conventional reporting. She didn't just cover stories—she lived inside them, embedding herself within the chaos of 1960s America while maintaining an acute sense of detachment. "We tell ourselves stories in order to live," she famously wrote, a line that encapsulates both her own search for meaning and her critique of a culture lost in its own narratives.

Her approach was immersive, deeply personal, and often unsettling. In *Slouching Towards Bethlehem*, she captured the fractured spirit of the era, particularly in the counterculture of Haight-Ashbury, where she spent time observing disillusioned youth drawn to the promise of revolution. Unlike other journalists who romanticized the movement, Didion saw its darker undercurrents—the aimlessness, the drug abuse, the unraveling of ideals. "The center was not holding," she wrote, echoing the foreboding tone of W.B. Yeats' poem *The Second Coming*, from which the book takes its name.

**Detached Yet Deeply Personal**

What made *Slouching Towards Bethlehem* revolutionary was Didion's ability to place herself within the story without making it about her. She was both observer and participant, someone who could stand amid the wreckage of 1960s idealism and coolly document its decay. "My only advantage as a reporter," she admitted, "is that I am so physically small, so temperamentally unobtrusive, and so neurotically inarticulate that people tend to forget that my presence runs counter to their best interests."

Yet, for all her detachment, the essays in *Slouching Towards Bethlehem* reveal a writer deeply affected by what she saw. In "Goodbye to All That," one of the book's most famous pieces, she reflects on her own youthful illusions about New York City, drawing a parallel between personal disillusionment and the broader cultural disillusionment of the time.

## The Legacy of *Slouching Towards Bethlehem*

Didion's impact on New Journalism—and on nonfiction writing in general—cannot be overstated. She proved that reporting could be deeply literary, that objectivity was not the only path to truth, and that personal voice could enhance, rather than diminish, credibility. "Style is character," she once said, and in *Slouching Towards Bethlehem*, her style—cool, precise, unflinching—became her signature.

More than five decades later, the book remains essential reading, not just for its portrait of a tumultuous era, but for its masterclass in storytelling. Didion wasn't just chronicling history—she was defining how we remember it.

## Defining a Style: Melding Personal Narrative with Cultural Critique

Joan Didion was never just a journalist, nor just a novelist. Her writing existed in a space where personal experience met sharp cultural critique, where the deeply subjective could illuminate broader societal truths. Her distinct voice—cool, precise, yet emotionally charged—set her apart from her contemporaries.

### Personal as Political

Didion's genius lay in her ability to connect the personal with the political, the intimate with the sweeping. "I'm not telling you to make the world better," she once wrote, "because I don't think that progress is necessarily part of the package. I'm just telling you to live in it. Not just to endure it, not just to suffer it, not just to pass through it, but to live in it." Her essays often began with her own experiences—her migraines, her anxieties, her observations about her surroundings—but always expanded into something larger.

In *The White Album* (1979), she famously wrote, "We live entirely, especially if we are writers, by the imposition of a narrative line upon disparate images." She understood that we don't just experience events; we shape them into stories that make sense of our world. This belief ran through her essays, where she used her own fragmented experiences to reflect the fragmented state of American culture.

**Detached Yet Devastating**

Didion's tone was often described as detached or clinical, but this was deceptive. Beneath the surface of her unflinching observations was a deep emotional core. Her signature style—short, declarative sentences, an almost forensic attention to detail—allowed her to expose the emptiness behind cultural myths.

Take her essay "Goodbye to All That," where she recalls her love affair with New York City and its inevitable disillusionment:

*"It is easy to see the beginnings of things, and harder to see the ends."*

She makes the reader feel the creeping loss, the quiet erosion of youthful idealism, not through sentimentality but through precision. Her cool detachment made the emotional weight of her words even stronger.

**A Mirror to American Culture**

Didion wasn't just writing about herself—she was writing about America. Whether dissecting the Hollywood mythmaking machine (*Play It As It Lays*), the instability of the counterculture (*Slouching Towards Bethlehem*), or the political unraveling of the country (*Salvador, Miami*), she always revealed how personal and national narratives intertwined.

She once described her role as a writer as someone who watches from the periphery:

*"I write entirely to find out what I'm thinking, what I'm looking at, what I see and what it means. What I want and what I fear."*

This introspection, combined with a journalist's eye for societal fault lines, defined her legacy. She didn't just report—she interrogated. She didn't just tell stories—she examined how and why we tell them.

Even today, her style remains unparalleled, her voice unmistakable. Joan Didion didn't just document her time—she captured the anxieties, contradictions, and illusions that continue to define American life.

## Establishing Credibility: Early Essays and Critical Acclaim

Before Joan Didion became a literary icon, she had to prove herself. She was a young woman writing in an industry dominated by men, carving out a space where her sharp observations and distinctive style could thrive. Her early essays, marked by an unsparing honesty and meticulous detail, laid the foundation for her credibility.

## The Power of Observation: "I Write Entirely to Find Out What I'm Thinking"

Didion's early essays revealed an intense focus on the nuances of American culture and personal experience. She believed that writing was an act of discovery, famously stating, *"I write entirely to find out what I'm thinking, what I'm looking at, what I see and what it means."* This self-reflective approach became one of her hallmarks.

Her breakthrough collection, *Slouching Towards Bethlehem* (1968), compiled many of her early essays, including "Some Dreamers of the Golden Dream," which chronicled the unraveling of a marriage in California's Inland Empire, and "On Keeping a Notebook," where she explored the personal nature of memory. Each essay combined journalistic precision with a novelist's introspection.

Critics took notice. The New York Times praised *Slouching Towards Bethlehem* as a work of *"precise, economical, and devastating prose."* The essays established Didion as a writer who could dissect both the personal and the cultural with surgical accuracy.

**The Craft of Unsentimental Storytelling**

Didion had an unmatched ability to write about deeply emotional subjects without falling into sentimentality. In her essay "Goodbye to All That," she documented her love affair with, and eventual disillusionment with, New York City.

*"I was in love with New York. I do not mean 'love' in any colloquial way. I mean that I was in love with the city, the way you love the first person who ever touches you and you never love anyone quite that way again."*

Her writing was deeply personal, yet universal, allowing readers to see their own experiences reflected in her words. The essay resonated with many, becoming one of her most celebrated pieces.

**Critical Acclaim and the Formation of a Literary Identity**

With *Slouching Towards Bethlehem*, Didion was no longer just a journalist—she was a literary force. She had a unique ability to blend keen social commentary with personal experience, a style that would define her career.

By the time she published *The White Album* (1979), her reputation as a formidable essayist was cemented. The opening line of the title essay became one of her most famous:

*"We tell ourselves stories in order to live."*

This single sentence encapsulated her entire approach to writing—examining the narratives we create, whether personal or cultural, to make sense of an often chaotic world.

Her early work established her as a writer who not only documented her time but shaped how we understood it. She had earned her credibility—not just as a journalist, but as one of the most incisive literary voices of her generation.

# Chapter 3: Expanding the Literary Landscape

## Novels that Captured a Generation: From "Run, River" to "Play It as It Lays"

While Joan Didion's essays made her a defining voice of her era, her novels carried an equal weight, offering stark portrayals of disillusionment, moral decay, and existential drift. From her debut novel *Run, River* (1963) to the haunting *Play It as It Lays* (1970), Didion's fiction captured the anxieties of a generation grappling with the unraveling of the American dream.

### A Cautious Beginning: *Run, River*

Didion's first novel, *Run, River*, was published when she was just 28. Set in her home state of California, it explored themes of power, identity, and personal failure through the story of a dysfunctional Sacramento family. Though she later admitted she wasn't entirely satisfied with the book, it set the stage for her lifelong preoccupation with the myths and illusions that shape American life.

*"I had written a novel about very real people who did not in fact seem real to me. This novel had been an exercise in things I had learned at Berkeley, a particular way of looking at things that I was not yet ready to question."*

The novel received modest attention, but it was clear that Didion's gift lay in her ability to expose the cracks beneath seemingly perfect surfaces.

## The Breakthrough: *Play It as It Lays*

Seven years later, Didion published *Play It as It Lays*, a novel that solidified her status as a major literary figure. It was a sharp, devastating portrayal of Hollywood's emotional emptiness, following Maria Wyeth, an actress whose life spirals into existential despair.

*"I know what 'nothing' means, and keep on playing."*

Maria's world is one of disconnection—fragments of conversations, empty relationships, and a relentless

California sun that exposes everything. Didion's prose in this novel was stripped down, mirroring Maria's emotional numbness.

*"What makes Iago evil? Some people ask. I never ask."*

With lines like these, Didion captured the nihilism of the late 1960s, an era defined by lost ideals and fading dreams. The novel resonated deeply, earning widespread critical acclaim.

**A Voice for a Disillusioned Generation**

Didion's novels weren't just fiction—they were time capsules of the cultural landscape. Her characters, often detached and adrift, reflected the broader anxieties of America in the wake of assassinations, war, and societal upheaval.

She once explained, *"Writing fiction is the act of discovering what you think."* And in *Play It as It Lays*, she revealed a deep understanding of a world where traditional narratives no longer held meaning.

By the time the novel was adapted into a film in 1972, Didion had cemented her place as a literary icon. She wasn't just chronicling a generation—she was giving it a voice.

## Memoirs and Essays: The Art of Personal and Political Storytelling

Joan Didion was a master of blending the personal with the political, transforming intimate experiences into larger cultural critiques. Through her essays and memoirs, she dissected the American psyche while exposing her own vulnerabilities. Whether reflecting on the unraveling of California in *The White Album* or mourning personal loss in *The Year of Magical Thinking*, Didion's work was always precise, unsentimental, and deeply affecting.

### Turning the Personal into the Political: *The White Album*

Didion's 1979 essay collection *The White Album* chronicled the chaos of the late 1960s, weaving her own life into the larger sociopolitical landscape. From the Manson murders to student protests, she observed history unfolding with a detached yet deeply personal lens.

*"We tell ourselves stories in order to live."*

This now-famous line from the title essay captures Didion's approach to writing—an attempt to find coherence in a world that often refuses to make sense. The essays in *The White Album* reveal a narrator who is both participant and observer, caught between the cultural upheaval of the time and her own struggles with anxiety and self-doubt.

### Grief as Narrative: *The Year of Magical Thinking*

Didion's most personal work, *The Year of Magical Thinking* (2005), chronicled the sudden death of her husband, John Gregory Dunne, and the near-fatal illness of their daughter, Quintana. Unlike her earlier essays, which often held emotion at a distance, this memoir was raw and deeply introspective.

*"Grief turns out to be a place none of us know until we reach it."*

Her prose in *The Year of Magical Thinking* was unembellished yet devastating, capturing the surreal and disorienting nature of loss. The book resonated with readers, winning the National Book Award and becoming a defining work on grief.

*"Life changes in the instant. The ordinary instant."*

Through Didion's meticulous chronicling of her mourning process, she made the deeply personal universal, proving once again that storytelling is not just about the self—it's about shared human experience.

Didion's memoirs and essays defined her as one of America's most important literary voices. Whether dissecting political landscapes or personal heartbreak, she remained committed to telling the truth, no matter how unsettling.

*"I have already lost touch with a couple of people I used to be."*

This reflection from *Slouching Towards Bethlehem* encapsulates the ever-evolving nature of identity—something Didion explored throughout her career. Her work, both personal and political, endures because of its unflinching honesty and razor-sharp insight into what it means to live, lose, and remember.

## Collaborative Screenwriting: The Didion-Dunne Partnership in Film

Joan Didion and her husband, John Gregory Dunne, formed one of Hollywood's most compelling screenwriting duos. Though Didion was best known for her essays and novels, her work in film showcased her sharp dialogue, economic storytelling, and ability to distill complex themes into emotionally charged narratives. Together, she and Dunne adapted novels, penned original scripts, and left a lasting impact on the film industry.

### Hollywood as a Business: A Pragmatic Approach to Screenwriting

Unlike her literary work, which was deeply personal, Didion viewed screenwriting as a profession rather than a passion. She once remarked:

*"Writing scripts is not writing. It's a different trade entirely."*

For Didion and Dunne, screenwriting was a way to support their writing careers, but it was also an exercise in discipline. While essays and novels allowed for creative introspection, film scripts required structure, brevity, and an understanding of commercial appeal.

## Adapting Literary Works: *Play It as It Lays* and *A Star Is Born*

One of their most notable adaptations was Didion's own novel, *Play It as It Lays* (1972), which explored existential despair and Hollywood's soulless underbelly. The adaptation captured the novel's fragmented structure and sense of alienation.

*"In a way, writing a screenplay is like designing a house someone else is going to live in. You know the structure, but it's out of your hands after that."*

Their script for *A Star Is Born* (1976), starring Barbra Streisand and Kris Kristofferson, was a high-profile project that required them to balance artistic integrity with studio demands. Didion and Dunne's draft gave depth to the story's themes of fame, self-destruction, and the cost of ambition, though the final version was heavily revised.

## Political Thrillers and Sharp Dialogue

Their most successful screenwriting effort was *The Panic in Needle Park* (1971), a gritty drama about heroin addiction starring Al Pacino in his first major film role. The screenplay was praised for its realism and understated dialogue—hallmarks of Didion's writing.

*"Let's just say we wanted to tell the truth without explaining it."*

Later, they tackled *True Confessions* (1981), a noir-inspired crime drama loosely based on the Black Dahlia murder. The script was dense with moral ambiguity, reflecting Didion's journalistic precision in depicting corruption and power.

## A Lasting Influence on Hollywood Storytelling

Though Didion never considered herself a "Hollywood writer," her work with Dunne proved that screenwriting, when done well, could be just as meticulous and impactful as literary writing. Their scripts, often minimalistic yet emotionally charged, set a precedent for nuanced storytelling in American cinema.

*"In Hollywood, you can survive almost anything—except being labeled 'difficult.'"*

Didion and Dunne's partnership exemplified a rare balance between art and commerce. While Didion's essays and novels remain her defining legacy, her contributions to film writing demonstrate her adaptability, precision, and unparalleled ability to capture human fragility in every medium.

# Chapter 4: The Art and Craft of Writing

## The Anatomy of a Sentence: Precision, Rhythm, and Detail

Joan Didion's prose is instantly recognizable—cool, controlled, and deceptively simple. Her writing is a masterclass in precision, rhythm, and detail, each sentence crafted with an almost surgical exactness. Didion's sentences do more than convey information; they create mood, evoke emotion, and reveal hidden truths. As she once put it:

> *"Grammar is a piano I play by ear, since I seem to have been out of school the year the rules were mentioned."*

This instinctive approach to language gave her work a distinctive rhythm, a balance between restraint and intensity that made even the smallest details resonate.

### Precision: Saying Exactly What Needs to Be Said

Didion believed that every word mattered. She stripped away excess, leaving behind only what was necessary. This precision was not just a stylistic choice—it was a philosophy. In her famous essay *Why I Write*, she explained:

> *"To shift the structure of a sentence alters the meaning of that sentence, as definitely and inflexibly as the position of a camera alters the meaning of the object photographed."*

She understood that sentence structure wasn't just about grammar; it was about perception. The way she arranged her words could subtly shift the reader's understanding, making her writing feel effortless yet deeply intentional.

## Rhythm: The Cadence of Thought

Didion's sentences often read like music, with a rhythm that propels the reader forward. Some are short and staccato, conveying urgency or detachment. Others stretch out, winding through layers of meaning. She played with repetition, pauses, and abrupt breaks, creating a style that felt both poetic and journalistic.

Consider the hypnotic repetition in *The White Album*:

> *"We tell ourselves stories in order to live. We interpret what we see, select the most workable of the multiple choices. We live entirely, especially if we are writers, by the imposition of a narrative line upon disparate images, by the 'ideas' with which we have learned to freeze the*

*shifting phantasmagoria which is our actual experience."*

The sentences build upon each other, mirroring the way the mind processes reality—grasping, reframing, and imposing order.

### Detail: The Power of the Specific

Didion's eye for detail was unmatched. She didn't just describe scenes; she captured the essence of a moment with an image so sharp it stayed with the reader long after the page was turned. She once said:

> *"The ability to think for one's self depends upon one's mastery of the language."*

Her details weren't decorative—they were meaning itself. In *Slouching Towards Bethlehem*, she describes a child in Haight-Ashbury:

> *"The five-year-old sits in front of a house on Pine Street in San Francisco eating a bar of hashish candy."*

There's no embellishment, no explanation—just the stark image. And that's what makes it powerful.

### Didion's Sentences as a Legacy

Didion's writing is a testament to the power of economy, rhythm, and detail. Her sentences, whether fragmented or flowing, are never accidental. Each one is a deliberate act of storytelling, a reflection of her unwavering belief that how we say something is just as important as what we say.

## Writing as Discovery: Reflections on the Creative Process

For Joan Didion, writing was not simply an act of recording thoughts—it was an act of discovery. She did not write because she had answers, but because she was searching for them. In her seminal essay *Why I Write*, she famously stated:

> *"I don't know what I think until I write it down."*

This encapsulated her approach to the craft. Writing was her way of making sense of the world, of structuring chaos into meaning. Her creative process was one of exploration, a constant unraveling of ideas, emotions, and memories through the act of putting words on paper.

### Writing as a Way of Thinking

Didion's essays and novels often feel like internal monologues, shaped by a mind that is both analytical and lyrical. She was not interested in simply stating opinions or recounting facts. Instead, her writing was an ongoing conversation with herself. She once described her process as an attempt to pin down fleeting thoughts:

> *"Had my credentials been in order I would*
> *never have become a writer. I had nothing to*
> *fall back on, and so I remained in the*
> *uncomfortable position of beginning again and*
> *again."*

She embraced the uncertainty of writing, understanding that a piece often took shape only as she wrote it. This idea is particularly evident in her nonfiction, where she follows tangents, examines contradictions, and allows the act of writing to guide her toward clarity.

**The Role of Observation**

Didion was, above all, an observer. She was known for her detached yet intimate style, carefully noting the small details that revealed larger truths. She described her process as almost obsessive, saying:

> *"You sit down at the typewriter and you put one*
> *word after another until it's done. It's that*
> *easy, and that hard."*

For Didion, writing was a discipline, one that required patience and precision. She spent hours staring at sentences, rearranging words, cutting anything unnecessary. The act of writing itself was what led her to understanding—not just about her subjects, but about herself.

## Writing as Control in a Chaotic World

Didion's work is often associated with themes of disorder—personal grief, political instability, cultural shifts. Yet, for her, writing was a means of regaining control. In *The Year of Magical Thinking*, written after the sudden death of her husband John Gregory Dunne, she used language to process her grief. She reflected:

> *"We tell ourselves stories in order to live."*

This wasn't just a statement about storytelling; it was a philosophy. Writing was how she navigated the unpredictability of life. It was how she imposed order on an otherwise chaotic world.

## Didion's Enduring Influence

Joan Didion's approach to writing—as an act of discovery, as a way of thinking, as a means of control—continues to influence writers today. Her belief that the process of writing shapes the thought itself remains a powerful testament to the craft. She never wrote to confirm what she already knew—she wrote to find out.

## Lessons from the Master: Interviews and Her Own Reflections

Joan Didion's insights about writing and life continue to inspire generations of writers. Throughout interviews and her reflective essays, she revealed that the act of writing was not merely a means to communicate ideas—it was an ongoing process of self-discovery and mastery. Didion once said,

> *"I write entirely to find out what I'm thinking, what I'm looking at, what I see and what it means."*

This declaration captures the essence of her creative process, suggesting that the act of putting thoughts into words was her primary tool for understanding the world and herself.

In conversations with fellow writers and in interviews like those conducted by The Paris Review, Didion often discussed how she learned the craft not from formal instruction alone but through constant experimentation and introspection. She approached writing with the precision of a surgeon and the intuition of an artist. Reflecting on her method, she remarked,

> *"Grammar is a piano I play by ear, since I seem to have been out of school the year the rules were mentioned."*

This playful yet profound observation highlights how she blended technical understanding with innate creativity. It was this balance that allowed her to transform everyday observations into lyrical, penetrating prose—a hallmark that has influenced countless writers.

Didion also emphasized the importance of embracing vulnerability in writing. She believed that a writer's strength lay in their willingness to expose their inner self. In one interview, she explained that writing was inherently an aggressive act of self-examination, stating,

> *"Writing is the act of imposing oneself upon the reader's most private space."*

By confronting her own emotions, memories, and uncertainties, Didion not only refined her voice but also created work that resonated on a deeply personal level with her audience. Her reflections encourage writers to be fearless, to let the act of writing reveal truths that even they might not have been aware of before.

Moreover, Didion's interviews reveal that she viewed the creative process as iterative—each draft, each sentence, a chance to discover a new nuance of meaning. She once described her work as "a high-wire act," where every word chosen was crucial in maintaining balance between clarity and emotion. This meticulous care in crafting sentences allowed her to capture the complexity of the human experience with startling clarity.

In sharing these lessons, Didion not only demystified the process of writing but also underscored the idea that great literature emerges from relentless curiosity and the courage to explore one's inner landscape. Her legacy, built on both her groundbreaking work and the wisdom imparted in her interviews, remains a beacon for those who seek to understand the art of storytelling from within.

# Chapter 5: Personal Life, Loss, and Memory

## Love, Marriage, and Dynamics with John Gregory Dunne

Joan Didion's marriage to John Gregory Dunne was far more than a personal union—it was a creative and intellectual partnership that deeply influenced her work. Their relationship bridged the gap between life and art, with each partner serving as a muse and collaborator. In a world where Didion was known for her cool reserve and meticulous prose, her bond with Dunne offered a rare glimpse of intimacy and shared creative spirit.

The couple met through mutual acquaintances and slowly built a connection that transcended conventional romance. They began as friends and gradually evolved into lifelong partners, both in marriage and in writing. Their collaboration on numerous screenplays and literary projects became a testament to how closely intertwined their personal and professional lives were. Didion's reflective nature found resonance in Dunne's equally probing insights, leading to a dynamic where ideas flowed freely between them. As she once put it,

> *"I write entirely to find out what I'm thinking, what I'm looking at, what I see and what it means."*

This declaration, though primarily about her writing process, also hints at the self-discovery fostered by their constant dialogue and shared experiences.

Their creative partnership was not without its challenges. Didion's famously reserved demeanor often contrasted with Dunne's more expressive style. Yet, it was this very contrast that enriched their work. Dunne was not only her husband but also her trusted editor and most candid critic. He championed her projects, helping refine her prose while their collaborative efforts on films like *Play It as It Lays* and *A Star Is Born* demonstrated their seamless ability to meld personal vision with commercial storytelling.

Despite the demands of public life and the pressures of the literary world, their relationship provided a steady foundation. They navigated life's turbulences together—from the exuberance of early success to the profound grief following personal losses. In their union, the blending of intellect and emotion became a source of strength, allowing Didion to explore themes of isolation, disillusionment, and memory with a unique clarity.

While Didion was often reluctant to reveal the inner workings of her personal life, the influence of her partnership with Dunne is unmistakable. Their joint journey was marked by a mutual respect for each other's talents and a shared commitment to the craft of writing. Their intertwined lives stand as a reminder that behind Didion's precise, sometimes enigmatic prose lay a deep and enduring connection—a bond that enriched her work and provided a wellspring of inspiration throughout her long and storied career.

## Confronting Grief: *The Year of Magical Thinking* and *Blue Nights*

Joan Didion's exploration of grief in her memoirs remains one of the most profound examinations of loss in contemporary literature. In *The Year of Magical Thinking*, she confronts the sudden, shattering loss of her husband, John Gregory Dunne, capturing the disorienting shock of bereavement with stark honesty. Didion writes,

> *"Life changes in the instant. The ordinary instant."*

These words encapsulate the abrupt rupture that grief imposes—a moment when the familiar is irrevocably transformed. In this work, Didion documents how she navigated a reality where every moment was infused with a haunting uncertainty. Her narrative is not merely a chronicle of loss; it is a meticulous exploration of the mind in crisis, where the act of writing becomes both a refuge and a means to understand the inexplicable. She reflects on the paradox of grieving, acknowledging that even as she sought to rationalize the unthinkable, part of her clung to magical thinking—a desperate hope that words might somehow restore what was lost.

In *Blue Nights*, Didion turns her gaze to the lingering grief over her daughter, Quintana Roo Dunne. While *The Year of Magical Thinking* grapples with an immediate, overwhelming shock, *Blue Nights* is a quieter, more reflective meditation on the slow, inexorable passage of time and the gradual erosion of what once was. Didion examines the intimate details of memory and loss, conveying the enduring pain of absence with a delicate, unsentimental clarity. As she ponders the process of aging and the relentless approach of mortality, she remarks on the persistent presence of grief—an ever-evolving companion that reshapes one's identity over time.

Didion's prose in both memoirs is characterized by a precise, almost surgical attention to language. Her reflections reveal that grief is not a linear process but a series of small, often imperceptible shifts in one's inner landscape. In confronting her loss, she writes not to find definitive answers, but to articulate the emotional terrain that grief forces one to traverse. Her meditative tone underscores the idea that storytelling, however painful, is essential for survival.

Together, *The Year of Magical Thinking* and *Blue Nights* form a dual testament to Didion's ability to transform personal anguish into literature that speaks to universal experiences. Through her unflinching honesty and evocative style, Didion reminds us that while grief may leave us fragmented, the act of writing can help us piece together a narrative of resilience and remembrance.

## Intimacy and Isolation: Diaries, Post-Therapy Notes, and Family Ties

Joan Didion's inner life was a landscape of intense intimacy juxtaposed with profound isolation—a duality that she captured in her diaries and post-therapy notes. Throughout her career, Didion maintained a meticulous record of her thoughts and feelings, a habit that allowed her to explore both personal vulnerability and the isolation that often accompanies creative genius.

Her diaries, long kept private, reveal a writer who used the act of recording her inner world as a means of understanding and survival. Didion once remarked,

> *"I write entirely to find out what I'm thinking, what I'm looking at, what I see and what it means."*

This credo underscores her approach to self-examination. Whether grappling with the fleeting moments of joy or the crushing weight of solitude, her writing served as a mirror to her soul, reflecting a mind constantly at work on its own identity.

The post-therapy notes—later compiled into the memoir *Notes to John*—offer an even more unvarnished glimpse into her struggles with anxiety, loss, and the often painful intricacies of family ties. In these intimate records, Didion dissected her emotions with the same precision that characterized her essays, using the written word to navigate the labyrinth of grief and isolation. These notes, left untouched until discovered after her death, testify to her belief that exposing one's vulnerabilities is both an act of courage and a necessary step toward healing.

Her family relationships, too, were a complex web of connection and distance. While she maintained close ties with those who mattered, Didion's observations about familial bonds often carried a note of detachment. She understood that deep connections sometimes come with a price: the loss of oneself amid the expectations and memories of others. Yet, it was this tension that fueled her literary work, allowing her to portray the bittersweet interplay between intimacy and isolation with uncanny clarity.

In one reflective moment, Didion observed that the stories we tell ourselves—about family, love, and loss—are essential to making sense of life. Her personal writings, whether in quiet diary entries or raw post-therapy notes, are testament to a life lived in perpetual dialogue with both the self and the people around her.

By laying bare her internal landscape, Didion not only charted her own journey through grief and connection but also provided readers with a powerful reminder: that even in isolation, our deeply personal stories connect us all.

# Chapter 6: Cultural Critique and the American Experience

## California as Muse: The Landscape, Myth, and Reality

For Joan Didion, California was never just a backdrop—it was a living, breathing muse that shaped her identity and informed her writing. Born and raised in Sacramento, Didion's deep connection to the Golden State emerged as both a personal touchstone and a vast canvas upon which she painted the contradictions of American life.

Didion saw California as a place where myth and reality intersected. The state's sun-soaked landscapes and its pioneering legacy became symbols of possibility and illusion. In her work, she captured the paradox of a land celebrated for its promise yet marked by a relentless erosion of ideals. "A place belongs forever to whoever claims it hardest, remembers it most obsessively, wrenches it from itself, shapes it, renders it, loves it so radically that he remakes it in his own image," she observed. This reflection speaks to the transformative power of California—a landscape that invites both adoration and critical scrutiny.

The sprawling deserts, the radiant coastlines, and the ever-changing urban vistas provided Didion with an endless array of images to explore. California's light, with its distinctive glare and shifting shadows, became a metaphor for the clarity and ambiguity in her own writing. It was a place that offered both a harsh reality and an alluring dreamscape. As she traveled its highways and byways, Didion absorbed every detail—the barren stretches that spoke of abandonment and the vibrant neighborhoods pulsing with cultural dynamism. Each element of the landscape was a clue to understanding the broader American narrative.

Yet, amid the mythic grandeur, Didion never lost sight of the everyday realities that defined California. She chronicled the state's contradictions: the glittering promise of Hollywood set against the stark loneliness of suburban sprawl; the bohemian ideals of the counterculture clashing with the relentless pragmatism of modern life. "We tell ourselves stories in order to live," she famously wrote, a line that encapsulates the way Californians—and Americans at large—construct narratives to reconcile their hopes with their disappointments.

For Didion, California was both an escape and a mirror. It was a realm where personal memory mingled with collective experience, offering a rich terrain for introspection and critique. Her essays often evoked the state's dual nature—the mythic promise of the West and its often brutal, unforgiving reality. This interplay between the imagined and the real is at the heart of her work, inviting readers to question the stories we tell about the places we call home.

In every line, Didion's writing reveals a profound awareness of California's power to inspire, disillusion, and ultimately transform those who live within its borders. Her legacy endures as a testament to the way a place can become an indelible part of one's soul, a source of endless narrative and meaning.

## Hollywood, Politics, and the Making of American Myths

Joan Didion was a consummate chronicler of American life, whose work penetrated the realms of Hollywood, politics, and the myths that shape national identity. Her incisive prose dismantled the polished facades of celebrity and political power, revealing the narratives behind the narratives.

In Hollywood, Didion observed a world of glamour and artifice. She dissected the film industry's mythology with a clinical precision that exposed its contradictions. Reflecting on the allure of cinema and the culture it both mirrored and manipulated, she noted,

> *"We tell ourselves stories in order to live."*
>
> This famous line encapsulates how Didion saw Hollywood's role: a realm where constructed images and carefully curated personas masked the underlying reality. While many were seduced by the promise of spectacle and success, Didion's writing

revealed the emptiness that often lay beneath the surface, making her a critical observer of a system driven more by myth than by substance.

Didion's commentary on politics was equally penetrating. She scrutinized how political figures and their campaigns crafted narratives to appeal to public sentiment. In her essays on American politics, she dissected the transformation of political discourse into a performance art—one that relies heavily on image and myth rather than policy. She observed the ways in which politicians, like Hollywood stars, were elevated to larger-than-life status, their every move staged for a captive audience. Her work laid bare the mechanics of a political system that favored style over substance, a system in which the power of narrative often outweighed the reality of governance.

By bridging the personal with the political, Didion transformed her observations into broader cultural critique. She recognized that American myths, whether born of Hollywood glamour or political theater, were essential constructs that helped people make sense of an increasingly complex world. As she reflected,

> *"It is our stories that define us, not the facts."*
> Though she rarely offered simple solutions, her keen insights compelled readers to question the narratives they accepted as truth.

Ultimately, Joan Didion's work in these arenas was not just about deconstructing myths—it was about understanding their power. Her unyielding analysis of the interplay between image and reality continues to challenge us to look beyond surface appearances and to scrutinize the stories we tell ourselves. In doing so, she carved a legacy as a writer who not only chronicled American culture but also shaped the conversation about what it means to live in a society built on storytelling.

# Observing a Nation: Essays on Society, Power, and the Media

## Observing a Nation: Essays on Society, Power, and the Media

Joan Didion's essays offer an unvarnished look at the fabric of American society. With a keen eye for detail and an incisive wit, she dissected the narratives that shape the nation's identity—examining how power is wielded, how media constructs reality, and how society tells itself stories to make sense of a chaotic world.

In works like *The White Album* and *Political Fictions*, Didion observed the shifting landscape of American politics and culture with a precision that was both clinical and deeply personal. "We tell ourselves stories in order to live," she famously declared, a line that encapsulates her belief that the narratives we construct are as vital as the facts themselves. Through her essays, she revealed that these stories—whether about political power, media spectacle, or social upheaval—often obscure the harsh realities beneath.

Didion's approach was not one of detached cynicism but of rigorous inquiry. She scrutinized the mechanics of media and the seductive power of political theater, noting how image and spectacle could shape public perception more effectively than hard evidence. Her essays exposed the gap between the grand narratives promoted by those in power and the disjointed, often disillusioned reality experienced by everyday Americans.

Her work on the media was particularly resonant. Didion noted that modern journalism often prioritizes style over substance, transforming complex issues into digestible snippets that, while compelling, could oversimplify critical truths. This critique is evident in her reflections on the "manufactured" nature of political discourse—where the media's role in creating and sustaining myths can sometimes be more influential than the actual events unfolding in the world.

At its core, Didion's body of work is a meditation on the interplay between perception and reality. She reminded readers that the stories we choose to believe have the power to define our collective experience. In her inimitable style, she challenged us to look beyond surface appearances and to question the narratives handed down by institutions, the press, and even our own memories.

Ultimately, Joan Didion's essays on society, power, and the media stand as a testament to her relentless pursuit of truth in an era defined by ambiguity. With unyielding clarity and poetic precision, she showed that understanding a nation requires not just an examination of facts, but an interrogation of the stories we tell about them.

# Chapter 7: Legacy, Archives, and Lasting Influence

## Honors, Awards, and Enduring Impact on American Letters

Joan Didion's career was not only defined by her incisive prose and cultural commentary but also by the recognition she received for her contributions to American literature. Her honors and awards serve as markers of her influence and a testament to the enduring power of her work.

Throughout her career, Didion amassed numerous accolades, including the National Book Award for *The Year of Magical Thinking*, which captured the raw emotions of loss and grief following her husband's sudden death. She also received the National Humanities Medal in 2013, an honor that acknowledged her unique ability to capture the spirit and contradictions of American life. Her work has been celebrated by institutions such as Harvard and Yale, which awarded her honorary Doctor of Letters, reflecting the academic and cultural significance of her contributions.

Didion's awards were not merely symbolic; they underscored the transformative impact of her writing. In her reflective style, she once stated,

*"We tell ourselves stories in order to live."*
This belief—that storytelling is central to understanding our own experiences and shaping collective memory—resonates deeply across her body of work. Her accolades thus become more than personal triumphs; they mark a literary legacy that continues to influence new generations of writers and thinkers.

Her ability to dissect the complexities of modern life, from the mythic landscapes of California to the intricacies of American politics and media, has left an indelible mark on American letters. Critics and peers alike have lauded her for reimagining nonfiction, transforming it into a powerful tool for cultural critique. As Didion herself explained,

> *"I write entirely to find out what I'm thinking, what I'm looking at, what I see and what it means."*
> This commitment to introspection and clarity helped her pioneer a style that is both lyrical and rigorously analytical.

Didion's work challenges readers to question the narratives that define their lives, inviting a deeper reflection on the forces that shape society. Her keen observations and distinctive voice have not only enriched literary discourse but also provided a framework for understanding the evolving American identity. Through her accolades and the widespread admiration of her peers, Didion's legacy endures as a touchstone for American literature—a reminder that powerful storytelling can illuminate the truths of our time.

In celebrating her achievements, we acknowledge a writer who transformed the art of narrative, leaving behind a legacy that continues to inspire and provoke thought long after the last page has been turned.

## The Didion-Dunne Archive: Preserving a Lifelong Journey

The Didion-Dunne Archive stands as a monumental repository of creative genius—a testament to the lifelong journey of two of America's most influential literary voices. Housed at the New York Public Library, this extensive collection preserves manuscripts, correspondence, photographs, and ephemera that chronicle the evolution of Joan Didion and John Gregory Dunne's intertwined careers.

This archive not only captures the polished final drafts of celebrated essays, novels, and screenplays but also unveils the raw, unfiltered materials of their creative process. It is in these marginal notes, personal letters, and early drafts that we glimpse the evolution of Didion's distinctive voice. As she famously stated,

> *"I write entirely to find out what I'm thinking, what I'm looking at, what I see and what it means."*

This conviction, evident in every piece of her work, is preserved in the archive's vast collection, providing scholars and readers a rare insight into how her ideas matured over decades. The archive is a living document of not just literary output, but of a dynamic partnership that saw Didion and Dunne exploring, refining, and sometimes challenging each other's perspectives.

Within these boxes are letters exchanged with notable figures—from fellow writers and critics to cultural icons—each correspondence shedding light on the broader context in which Didion's work was created. These documents underscore her belief that storytelling is not only about recording events but about interpreting the world, echoing her observation,

*"We tell ourselves stories in order to live."*

The Didion-Dunne Archive encapsulates a journey marked by constant reinvention and relentless pursuit of truth. It preserves the legacy of a writer who never ceased to dissect the narratives that define both personal and collective realities. For Didion, every piece of writing was an exploration—a quest to understand the subtle interplay of memory, language, and perception.

By making these materials accessible to future generations, the archive ensures that the creative spirit of Didion and Dunne endures. It is an invaluable resource for anyone seeking to understand not only the history of American letters but also the intimate process of crafting stories that resonate deeply with the human experience.

In preserving these artifacts, the Didion-Dunne Archive honors the profound impact of a partnership that transformed the landscape of American literature. It is a reminder that behind every celebrated work lies a complex, often painstaking journey of discovery—a journey that continues to inspire, challenge, and inform readers and writers alike.

## Posthumous Revelations: New Publications and the Continuing Conversation

Since her passing, new publications have shed fresh light on Joan Didion's creative mind, inviting readers to engage with her work in new and unexpected ways. Posthumous releases, such as *Notes to John*, offer an intimate glimpse into her internal dialogues, chronicled in a series of diary entries and post-therapy notes discovered among her personal papers. In these raw reflections, Didion's relentless quest for understanding is palpable. She once explained,

> *"I write entirely to find out what I'm thinking, what I'm looking at, what I see and what it means."*

This credo remains at the heart of her newly revealed writings, allowing audiences to trace the evolution of her thoughts long after the public persona was established.

The publication of *Notes to John*—a collection of entries addressed to her late husband, John Gregory Dunne—has sparked a continuing conversation among scholars and fans. It serves as a bridge between Didion's public works and her private introspection, illustrating how the process of writing was not just a creative endeavor, but a way to navigate the depths of grief, memory, and identity. As Didion famously observed,

*"We tell ourselves stories in order to live."*

This insight now gains even more significance in the context of her posthumous revelations, inviting readers to reconsider the narratives she constructed about life, loss, and the passage of time.

Moreover, ongoing efforts to digitize and make accessible the Didion-Dunne Archive have further enriched the discussion surrounding her legacy. The archive, which preserves not only polished essays and novels but also early drafts, letters, and personal notes, continues to offer new perspectives on her meticulous creative process. Each newly released document reinforces the idea that Didion's work was a constant negotiation between the personal and the cultural, the spontaneous and the meticulously crafted.

In the wake of these new publications, literary critics and enthusiasts are engaging in a vibrant dialogue about Didion's influence on American letters. Her unyielding honesty, precise language, and capacity to capture the complexities of modern life continue to inspire both established writers and emerging voices. As the conversation evolves, Didion's words remind us that her legacy is not confined to the pages of her books; it lives on in the continuing effort to understand and articulate the human experience.

The posthumous revelations thus open a new chapter in the Didion narrative—a chapter that honors her past contributions while inviting future generations to explore the intricate interplay of memory, storytelling, and the relentless pursuit of truth.

# Conclusion

Joan Didion's work stands as a monument to the power of storytelling—a testament to the capacity of language to capture the elusive truths of our lives and our culture. In exploring her life, from her Sacramento roots to the multifaceted career that spanned essays, novels, screenplays, and memoirs, we have witnessed a writer who dared to expose both the fragility of the human condition and the complex narratives that define our society.

Didion's journey from a precocious child in California to one of America's most influential literary voices reflects her unyielding commitment to examining the world with unflinching clarity. Whether it was her groundbreaking contributions to New Journalism in *Slouching Towards Bethlehem*, her haunting explorations of grief in *The Year of Magical Thinking* and *Blue Nights*, or her incisive critiques of Hollywood and politics, Didion's work remains as relevant as ever. She taught us that the stories we tell are essential to our very survival. As she famously asserted,

*"We tell ourselves stories in order to live."*

This idea, echoing throughout her writings, invites us to question the narratives that shape our reality and to recognize the transformative power of personal and cultural storytelling.

Her partnership with John Gregory Dunne further exemplified the beauty of collaboration—a union that blended the personal with the professional to create works that challenged and redefined cultural boundaries. Their joint projects in film and literature reveal how deeply interconnected the realms of art and life can be when navigated with passion, precision, and mutual respect.

Moreover, the revelations from Didion's diaries, post-therapy notes, and the comprehensive Didion-Dunne Archive remind us that behind every celebrated work lies a complex, often private, process of discovery. Didion's meticulous attention to language and detail—her belief that

*"I write entirely to find out what I'm thinking, what I'm looking at, what I see and what it means"*

—continues to inspire writers and readers alike to explore the hidden depths of their own experiences.

As we close this exploration of Joan Didion's enduring legacy, we are left with a profound understanding that her work transcends mere documentation of a time or a place. Instead, it captures the very essence of what it means to live, to observe, and to create meaning in a world that is both beautiful and brutal. Her literary voice—a blend of personal introspection, cultural critique, and unyielding honesty—remains a beacon for all who seek to understand the interplay between memory, myth, and reality.

In celebrating Joan Didion, we honor a writer whose legacy is as much about the courage to confront life's uncertainties as it is about the art of storytelling itself. Her words continue to challenge us, inspire us, and remind us that in the end, it is our stories that define who we are.

# References

1. **Joan Didion: About Joan Didion.**

   Retrieved from

   https://www.joandidion.org/about-joan-didion

2. **The Didion Dunne Archive at the New York Public Library.**

   Retrieved from

   https://www.joandidion.org/didion-dunne-new-york-public-library-archive

3. **Grimes, William. "Joan Didion, 'New Journalist' Who Explored Culture and Chaos, Dies at 87."**

   *The New York Times*, December 23, 2021.

   Retrieved from

   https://www.nytimes.com/2021/12/23/books/joan-didion-dead.html

4. **Clark, Alex. "Joan Didion, American Journalist and Author, Dies at Age 87."** *The Guardian*, December 23, 2021. Retrieved from https://www.theguardian.com/books/2021/dec/23/joan-didion-american-journalist-and-author-dies-at-age-87

5. **Achievement.org – Joan Didion.** Retrieved from https://achievement.org/achiever/joan-didion/

6. **Didion, Joan – The Art of Fiction No. 71.** *The Paris Review*, Fall-Winter 1978. Retrieved from https://www.theparisreview.org/interviews/3439/the-art-of-fiction-no-71-joan-didion

7. **We Tell Ourselves Stories: Joan Didion and the American Dream Machine.** Marc Weingarten, *Los Angeles Times*, March 10, 2025.

Retrieved from

https://www.latimes.com/entertainment-arts/book
s/story/2025-03-10/joan-didion-we-tell-ourselves-st
ories-john-wayne-alissa-wilkinson

8. **"25 Years Ago, Joan Didion Kept a Diary. It's
   About to Become Public."**

   *The New York Times*, February 5, 2025.

   Retrieved from

   https://www.nytimes.com/2025/02/05/books/ne
   w-book-joan-didion-notes-to-john.html

9. **Hanging Out With Joan Didion: What I
   Learned About Writing From an American
   Master.**

   Sara Davidson, *Literary Hub*, October 5, 2021.

   Retrieved from

   https://lithub.com/hanging-out-with-joan-didion-
   what-i-learned-about-writing-from-an-american-m
   aster/

10. **Joan Didion: Why I Write.**

*Literary Hub*, January 26, 2021.

Retrieved from

https://lithub.com/joan-didion-why-i-write/

*Note: Additional biographical details and internal citations (e.g., references within Didion's works) are drawn from the comprehensive texts provided and her own published writings. All excerpts and quotes are used in accordance with fair use principles, with proper attribution to the original sources.*

Made in the USA
Middletown, DE
12 May 2025

75430000R00049